D1127349

THE TRUE JIHAD

Also by Maulana Wahiduddin Khan

Islam Rediscovered

Islam and Peace

God Arises

Islam As It Is

God-Oriented Life

A Treasury of the Qur'an

Woman in Islamic Shari'ah

Words of the Prophet Muhammad

Islam: The Voice of Human Nature

Muhammad: A Prophet for All Humanity

THE TRUE JIHAD

The Concepts of Peace, Tolerance and Non-Violence in Islam

Maulana Wahiduddin Khan

Presenting Islam in the context of modern times

First published 2002

Goodword Books Pvt. Ltd.
1, Nizamuddin West Market
New Delhi-110 013
Tel. 9111-4355454, 4356666
Fax 9111-4357333, 4357980
info@goodwordbooks.com

TABLE OF CONTENTS

بسم الله الرحمن الرحيم

Preface

A perusal of the Qur'an followed by a study of latter-day Muslim history will reveal a blatant contradiction between the two—that of principle and practice. Where recent developments in some Muslim countries bespeak the culture of war, the Qur'an, on the contrary, is imbued with the spirit of tolerance. Its culture is not that of war, but of mercy.

At the very beginning of the Qur'an, the first invocation reads: "In the name of God, the most Merciful, the most Beneficent." Throughout the Qur'an, God's name is thus invoked no less than 113 times. Moreover, the Qur'an states that the prophets were sent to the world *as a mercy to the people* (21:107).

The word '*jihad*' has nowhere been used in the Qur'an to mean war in the sense of launching an offensive. It is used rather to mean 'struggle'. The action most consistently called for in the Qur'an is the exercise of patience. Yet today, the 'Muslim Mujahideen' under unfavourable conditions have equated "God is Great" with "War is Great." For them, the greatest reward is to be able to wield a Kalashnikov rifle.

In the light of on-going conflict, we must ask why so great a contradiction has arisen between the principles of Islam and the practices of Muslims. At least one root cause may be traced to historical exigency.

Since time immemorial, military commanders have been accorded positions of great eminence in the annals of history. It is a universal phenomenon that the hero is idolized even in peace time and becomes a model for the people. It is this placing of heroism in the militaristic context which has been the greatest underlying factor in the undue stress laid on war in the latter phase of Islam's history. With the automatic accord in Muslim society of a place of honour and importance to the heroes of the battlefield, annalists' subsequent compilations of

Islamic history have tended to read like an uninterrupted series of wars and conquests.

These early chronicles having set the example, subsequent writings on Islamic history have followed the same pattern of emphasis on militarism. The Prophet's biographies were called *maghazi*, that is, 'The Battles Fought by the Prophet,' yet the Prophet Muhammad ﷺ in fact did battle only three times in his entire life, and the period of his involvement in these battles did not total more than one and a half days. He fought, let it be said, in self-defence, when hemmed in by aggressors, where he simply had no option. But historians—flying in the face of fact—have converted his whole life into one of confrontation and war.

We must keep it in mind that the Prophet Muhammad ﷺ was born at a time when an atmosphere of militancy prevailed in Arab society, there being, in their view, no other path to justice. But the Prophet always opted for avoidance of conflict. For instance, in the campaign of Ahzab, the Prophet advised his Companions to dig a trench between them and the enemies, thus preventing a head-on clash.

Another well-known instance of the Prophet's dislike for hostilities is the Hudaibiyyah peace treaty in which the Prophet accepted all the conditions of the enemy. In the case of the conquest of Makkah, he avoided a battle altogether by making a rapid entry into the city with ten thousand Muslims—a number large enough to awe his enemies into submission.

In this way, on all occasions, the Prophet endeavoured to achieve his objectives by peaceful rather than by war-like means. It is, therefore, unconscionable that in later biographical writing, all the events of his life have been arranged under the heading of 'battles' (*ghazawat*). How he managed to avert the cataclysms of war has not been dealt with in any of the works which purportedly depict his life.

Ibn Khaldun, the celebrated 14th century historian, was the first to lay down definite rules for the study and writing of history and sociology. He followed the revolutionary course of attempting to present history as a chronicle of events centering on the common man rather than on kings, their generals and the battles they fought. But since war heroes were already entrenched as the idols of society, the caravan of writers and historians continued to follow the same well-worn path as had been trodden prior to Ibn Khaldun. When people have come to regard war heroes as the greatest of men, it is but natural that it is the events of the battlefield which will be given the greatest prominence in works of history. All other events will either be relegated to the background or omitted altogether.

In the past when the sword was the only weapon of war, militancy did not lead to the mass-scale loss of life and property such as modern warfare brings in its wake. In former times, fighting was confined to the battlefield; the only sufferers were those engaged in the battle. But today, the spear and sword have been replaced by megabombs and devastating long-range missiles, so that killing and destruction take place on a horrendous scale. It is the entire human settlement which has now become the global arena of war. Even the air we breathe and the water we drink are left polluted in war's aftermath.

Hence people in the West find Islam outdated and irrelevant precisely because of its militant interpretation. Demands for a reform in Islam are on the increase, as the 'old' version of Islam cannot apparently keep pace with the modern world.

But, in reality, it is not reformation which is urgent, but revival. What is needed is to discard as superficial and erroneous the militant and political interpretation of Islam, and to adopt the original, 'old' version of Islam based on peace, mercy and the love of mankind.

The so-called Muslim Mujahideen have been exhorting their co-religionists to do battle all over the world. But the Qur'an says: '...and God calls to the home of peace' (10:25). It is up to right-thinking people everywhere to reject the militant version of Islam, and to start seeing and accepting Islam as it is truly represented by the Qur'an.

Wahiduddin Khan

The Islamic Centre, New Delhi
January 4, 2002

THE TRUE JIHAD

"Read! In the name of your Lord..."
(The Quran, 96:1)

The Quran exhorts believers to "strive for the cause of Allah as it behoves you to strive for it." (22:78) This earnest struggle is expressed in Arabic by the word *'jihad'* which is derived from the root '*juhd*', which means to strive, to struggle, that is, to exert oneself to the utmost to achieve one's goal.

Thus the original meaning of *jihad* in Arabic is striving very hard'. Since the early Muslims had to strive hard during wars with aggressors, these wars came, in an extended sense, to be called jihad. However, the actual word for such a war in Arabic is *qital,* not *jihad.*

War with an aggressor is a chance occurrence, taking place as warranted by particular situations, while *jihad* is a continuous action which is at the core of the believer's life day in and day out. It is an ongoing process. This constant *jihad* means strict adherance to the will of God in all aspects of one's life, and the prevention of any obstacle coming in the way of fulfilling God's will—for instance, the desires of the self, the urge to serve one's own interests, the compulsion of social traditions, the need for compromises, ego problems, greed for wealth, etc. All these things directly thwart righteous actions. Overcoming all such hurdles and persevering in obeying God's commands are the real *jihad*. And the word *jihad* has been used primarily in this sense. We quote here some traditions, as recorded in Musnad Ahmad, which define the role of the *mujahid*.

1. A *mujahid* is one who struggles with himself for the sake of God. (6/20)

2. A *mujahid* is one who exerts himself for the cause of God (6/22)

3. A *mujahid* is one who struggles with his self in submission to the will of God.

The present world is a testing ground: the entire fabric of this world has been designed with a view to fulfilling the purposes of the divine trial of man. This being so, the human being is necessarily faced with all kinds of temptations, which are so many barriers to his measuring up to God's standards. For instance, when a matter of truth comes before him and he fails to acknowledge it for fear of losing his status; when he has someone's wealth or property in his possession, and he hesitates about restoring it to the true owner; when he resents having to place curbs on himself in order to lead a life of modesty as desired by God; when he feels that suppressing his anger and vengefulness in order to be patient amounts to his own negation; when he fails to speak words of truth and stand up for justice for fear of losing his popularity; when he is loath to renounce comforts and convenience, etc., in order to be of a principled character instead of a selfish character. On all such occasions man has to curb his desires. It becomes essential for him to sacrifice his feelings. At times he may feel that he

Islamic jihad is a positive and continuous process. It is at work in the entire life of a believer.

has to kill his ego completely. In spite of having to surmount all such hurdles, the individual should be determined to stick to the truth in the real and primary sense of jihad. Those who engage in this *jihad* will be held deserving of paradise in the Hereafter.

'Jihad' essentially is a peaceful struggle. One form of this peaceful struggle is *dawah* (communication of the message of God).

The Quran States:

> *Do not yield to the unbelievers, but fight them strenuously with it (the Quran) (25:52).*

No military activity is referred to in this verse of the Quran. We are not meant to engage in physical combat with the non-believers. What this verse actually means is that we must engage ourselves in *dawah* activities through the teachings of the Quran, that is, striving ourselves to the utmost on an ideological plane, while sifting truth from falsehood.

Even in the face of a military challenge from the enemy, all efforts will be made to counter aggression by peaceful methods. The path of peace can be abandoned only when it has become impossible to stick to it, and only when there is no other option but to give a military response in self-defence.

A tradition narrated by Aisha, the Prophet's wife, provides a guiding principle. She said: Whenever the Prophet had to choose between two courses, he would always opt for the easier one. This means that whenever the Prophet had two options before him in any matter, he would always abandon the harder option in favour of the easier one (Bukhari).

Whenever the Prophet had to choose between two courses, he would always opt for the easier course.

This tradition (*sunnah*) of the Prophet Muhammad ﷺ is relevant not only to everyday affairs but also to such serious matters as, by their very nature, relate to harder options.

The study of the Prophet's life shows that he never initiated a military move himself. When his opponents wanted to embroil him in war, he would on all occasions apply some strategy of avoidance to avert war. He fought only when there was no other way left to him. According to the *sunnah* of the Prophet, there is no aggressive or offensive war in

Islam. Islam allows only a defensive war and that, too, only when there is no other option.

The truth is that in life we have to face the problem of choosing between two courses: between the confrontational and the non-confrontational, between the peaceful and the violent. The study of the Prophet's life tells us that the Prophet, in all matters, abandoned the violent or confrontational course in favour of the peaceful or non-confrontational course. The whole life of the Prophet provides a successful, practical example of this principle. We give here some examples of this nature.

1. After being appointed as Prophet, the first question before him was which of the two above-mentioned courses he should follow. As we know, the Prophet's mission was to bring polytheism *(shirk)* to an end and establish monotheism in its place. The Kabah in Makkah had already been established as a centre of monotheism, but at the time of the Prophet 360 idols were already installed within its walls. In view of this situation, the first verses to be revealed in the Quran should have been

to this effect: "Purify the Kabah of all idols," and then, after making it a centre of *tawhid* or oneness of Allah, work for your mission.

But beginning his mission with this task would have amounted to waging war, for it was the Quraysh who were the guardians of the Kabah as the well as the leaders of Arabia.

The Prophet therefore totally avoided the physical purification of the Kabah and limited himself to the theoretical communication of the message of monotheism. It was the first prophetic example of adopting a peaceful and non-confrontational method instead of a violent or confrontational method.

The entire life of the Prophet is a practical demonstration of his peace-loving policy.

2. Adhering strictly to this peaceful principle, the Prophet continued to work in Makkah for a period of thirteen years. But even then, the Quraysh turned his dire enemies. Ultimately, the Quraysh's leaders in consultation among themselves arrived at a consensus to kill the Prophet. Therefore, armed youths of their tribe surrounded his home one night to put their plan into action.

This was an open challenge for the Prophet and his companions to do battle with them. Instead, the Prophet guided by God, decided to avoid any military encounter. Therefore, in the stillness of the night, he quietly left his home in Makkah for Madinah. This event is called the emigration (*hijrah*) in the history of Islam. Emigration is a clear example of abandoning violent solutions in favour of peaceful solutions.

Migration or hijrah of the Prophet Muhammad is a clear example of abandoning violent solutions in favour of peaceful solutions.

3. The battle of the Trench is another example of this *sunnah* of the Prophet. On this occasion a large number of people from different tribes had come to Madinah with the intention of attacking it. It was clearly a military challenge. But the Prophet used strategy to avoid an encounter with the enemy. According to this plan, the Prophet worked hard day and night along with his companions to dig a long trench between him and his opponents. This trench served as a buffer.

Therefore, when the army of the Quraysh arrived, they could not attack. So they camped there for some days. In the end they gave up the idea of attacking as it was impossible to cross the ditch. They eventually left Madinah. The digging of this trench provides an example of opting for a peaceful course instead of a violent course.

4. The Hudaybiyya peace treaty also provides another example of this sunnah of the Prophet. At that time the Prophet and his companions had wanted to perform the minor pilgrimage *(umrah)* by entering Makkah. But when they reached Hudaybiyya, which was nine miles from Makkah, they were stopped by the Quraysh leaders. They said that in no event would they allow them to enter Makkah. This again was a military challenge. If the Prophet wanted to advance as planned towards Makkah, an encounter was sure to take place. Therefore, the Prophet ended his journey at Hudaybiyya and entered into a peace treaty, accepting unilaterally the conditions laid down by the enemy. He then came back to Madinah without having performed the umrah. This was a very clear prophetic

example of adopting a peaceful method as opposed to a violent method.

5. The conquest of Makkah provides an equally telling example of this same *sunnah*. At that time the Prophet was accompanied by 10,000 devoted followers. They could certainly have fought a successful battle with the Quraysh, yet the Prophet Muhammad ﷺ decided to demonstrate his power rather than use it. He did not come out with his 10,000 strong army to declare war against the Quraysh in order to conquer Makkah after a bloody encounter. He instead made preparations for a journey with the utmost secrecy, and travelling with his companions, he quietly entered Makkah. This entry was so sudden that the Quraysh could not make any preparations for war and Makkah was conquered without any carnage. This incident provides a fine example of adopting a peaceful instead of a violent method. These examples show that not only in normal

As seen during the conquest of Makkah, the Prophet adhered to the principle of peace even in extreme emergencies.

situations but also in extreme emergencies the Prophet adhered to the principle of peace rather than that of war. All his successes are practical examples of this sunnah of peace.

6. As mentioned above, the position of peace in Islam is sacrosanct, while war in Islam is allowed only in exceptional cases when it cannot be avoided. Granted that this is so, let us look at the state of affairs prevailing today. This modern age is totally different from preceding centuries. In ancient times violence was the norm, so that maintaining the peace was extremely difficult. But now the situation has totally changed. Today, we have reached the ultimate stage where any kind of violence is undesirable or unacceptable. Indeed, a peaceful strategy is the only viable solution. Furthermore, in our times a peaceful course of action is backed up by ideological and practical arguments, which invest it with all the greater power and sanctity.

Far from being an armed struggle, jihad is a peaceful struggle.

These modern support systems have a number

of very positive aspects, for instance, the right to freedom of expression, the possibilities opened up by the communications system of spreading one's message across the globe, etc. These modern changes have rendered possible a peaceful course of action, which has far greater popularity and is at the same time more effective.

Now, a peaceful course of action is not just one of the possibilities: it is the only feasible and result-oriented option.

As mentioned above, the *sunnah* or way of the Prophet is that, if it is possible to adopt a peaceful method, it should be put into practice during any Islamic struggle. A violent course of action should be shunned altogether. Now the present state of affairs is that, as a result of the changes that have taken place in the present age, the peaceful method is not only available at all times but, due to various supporting factors, has become the most effective course of action. It would therefore be no exaggeration to say that in present times a violent struggle is not only a hard option but is not in practice useful. Whereas non-violence is not only an easier option, but is also highly effective and result-oriented. Now, a peaceful course of action is not just one of the possibilities: it is the only feasible and result-oriented option. This being so, it would be right to say that violence has been practically abandoned. This is what we call an abrogated command in the language of the *shariah* (Islamic law). Now believers are, in reality, left with only one choice, and that is indeed the peaceful course of action.

In recent times, one celebrated example of the success of such a course is to be found in the life of the Indian leader, Mahatma Gandhi (d.1948). Due to temporal changes, it became possible for Mahatma Gandhi to wage political battles successfully by adopting the principle of non-violence and engaging in peaceful activism in the full sense of these expressions.

It is a known principle that the commands of the *shariah* change according to altered situations. This accepted principle of *fiqh* (Islamic jurisprudence) demands that with the changing times, a new application of the *shariah* should be sought in order that *shariah* commands may be in consonance with the changing circumstances.

This principle of Islamic jurisprudence relates not only to civic matters, but also certainly to the waging of war. This principle demands the practical avoidance of a violent course of action. Only a peaceful course of action should be accorded the status of a *shariah* command.

The Jihad Movements of Modern Times

According to the Islamic shariah, peace is the rule in matters of jihad, while war is the least desirable option.

It is true that in ancient times violent solutions were adopted at certain stages due to the prevailing circumstances. Opponents had no other alternative. Now, with the changing of the times, there is no longer this compulsion. Therefore, launching out on a violent course of action is not only unnecessary, but also unIslamic. In these modern times non-violent conduct is the best option.

According to the Islamic *shariah*, peace is the rule in matters of *jihad*, while war is the least desirable option.

In present times groups of Muslims in many countries have launched movements of armed *jihad*, in the name of Islam. But a movement cannot be a *jihad* just because its leaders describe it as such.

An action can be termed a *'jihad'* only when it fulfills the conditions set by Islam. Any military action which is carried out without fulfilling these conditions will not be a *jihad* but a *fasad*, which will amount to spreading corruption across the world. Those who engage in such a *'jihad'* will not deserve any reward. They should expect only divine punishment.

The special conditions of *jihad* have been dealt with in detail in the following chapter. Here I would like to lay stress on one important aspect of it. That is, *jihad* in the sense of *qital* (armed struggle) does not fall into the same category of individual acts of devotion as prayer and fasting: it is an activity which relates totally to the state.

The true Islamic *jihad* as it relates to the

individuals is a positive and continuous process, which is at work throughout the entire life of a believer. There are three major kinds of this process of *jihad*.

1. *Jihad-e-nafs:* to control one's negative and undesirable feelings within oneself and to persevere in the life of God's choice in all circumstances.

'Jihad' essentially is a peaceful struggle. One form of this peaceful struggle is dawah (communication of the message of God)

2. *Dawah jihad:* to communicate the message of God to all human beings and deal with all human beings with full compassion and well-wishing. This is a gigantic task. That is why it has been called the greatest *jihad* in the Quran.

3. *Jihad* with antagonists: to counter any challenge from the opponents of religion, and to safeguard religion in all circumstances. This *jihad* basically has always been a peaceful process, and it is still so even today. In this respect, far from being an armed offensive, *jihad* is essentially a peaceful struggle.

PEACE IN THE QURAN

"God calls to the Home of Peace."
(The Quran, 10:25)

At a three-day symposium held at the American University in Washington, on Feb 1998, I made a speech on "Islam and Peace", a part of which is given below:

"It is no exaggeration to say that Islam and violence are contradictory to each other. The concept of Islamic violence is so obviously unfounded that prima facie it stands rejected. The fact that violence is not sustainable in the present world is sufficient indication that violence as a principle is quite alien to the scheme of things in Islam. Islam claims to be an eternal religion and, as such, could never afford to uphold any principle which could not stand up to the test of time. Any attempt to bracket violence

The truth is that Islam's being a peaceful religion shows that it is an eternal religion. Had it been a religion of violence, it would not have stood the test of time.

with Islam amounts, therefore, to casting doubt upon the very eternity of the Islamic religion. Islamic terrorism is a contradiction in terms, much like 'pacifist' terrorism. And the truth of the matter is that, all the teachings of Islam are based directly or indirectly on the principle of peace."

The Teachings of Islam

The very word 'Islam' (from the Arabic *silm*) connotes peace. According to a tradition of the Prophet, 'Peace is Islam' *(Al-Bukhari)*. This means that peace is one of the prerequisites of Islam. Similarly, a *hadith* states: A Muslim is one from whose tongue and hands people are safe. One of the attributes of God described in the Quran is *'As-Salam'*, which means peace and security.' That is to say that God's Being itself is a manifestation of peace. Indeed, God is Peace *(Al-Bukhari)*. In the Quran divine guidance is likened to the paths of peace. (5:16)

According to Islam, Paradise is the ideal human abode, and is thus called the 'Home of Peace.' It is also said that, the people of Paradise will wish peace to one another, indicating that the social culture of the people of Paradise will be based on peace.

The Quran, avers that, 'reconciliation is best' (4:128), and judging by the consequences, the way of peace is far better than that of confrontation. By the law of Nature, God has decreed that success will be met with only on a reconciliatory path, and not on a confrontational or a violent course of action.

The position of peace in Islam is sacrosanct, while war in Islam is allowed only in exceptional cases when it cannot be avoided.

Whenever the Prophet had an option between two courses of action, he always chose the easier (non-confrontational) one. *(Bukhari)*

This means that, violent activism should not be indulged in if peaceful activism is an option. For, peace is the easier course as compared to violence.

For instance, trying to change the status quo in the very first stage of a movement is a hard option, while launching one's activities in the available sphere without doing so is an easier option.

Going to war in confrontational situations is a hard option while following a conciliatory course in dealing with one's rival is easier. Countering aggression with aggression is a hard option, while countering aggression with patience and forbearance is an easier option. An agitational course of action is harder than employing quiet strategy. Adopting a radical method of reformation is harder than that of following a gradual method. Taking emotional, extreme steps without a thought for their consequences creates difficulties. While a well-considered method, keeping an eye on the consequences, gives much better results. The policy of confrontation with a ruler is a harder option,

Countering aggression with aggression is a hard option, while countering aggression with patience and forbearance is an easier option.

while initiating one's action, by side-stepping the ruler in the sphere of education and learning is an easier option. These instances show us the easier and harder options, as demonstrated by the Hadith.

The truth is that peace in Islam is the 'rule', while war is the 'exception'. This is borne out by all the teachings of Islam and the practical life of the Prophet of Islam.

THE EXAMPLE OF THE PROPHET MUHAMMAD ﷺ

The Prophet Muhammad ﷺ received his first revelation in 610 in Makkah. God ordained that he carry out the mission of *tawhid* (or oneness of Allah).

The house of the Kabah, which was built as the house of monotheism by the Prophet Ibrahim عليه السلام and his son Ismail, later on became a centre of polytheism with 360 idols in it. The first revelation might well have demanded the purification of the Kabah, which would have given rise to a serious problem. But the first revelation made in the Quran was: Purify your vestments (74:4). This means to purify one's moral character. If, in the first stage the

Prophet had been commanded to purify the Kabah while Makkah was still under the domination of the idolaters, this would have surely precipitated clash and confrontation. Therefore, according to the command of the first revelation, the Prophet continued to perform his prayers peacefully in the Kabah for a period of 13 years, even though it housed several hundred idols.

The goal of the Islamic mission is to make people realize the existence of the one and only God and to strive to bring about a revolution in their hearts and minds.

Similarly, the Prophet and his companions circumambulated the Kabah on the occasion of Umrah al-Hudaybiyya in 629, while the Kabah still housed 360 idols.

The Prophet Muhammad ﷺ proceeded thus in order to avoid war and confrontation with the idolaters, and so that the atmosphere of peace should be maintained. The entire life of the Prophet is a practical demonstration of this peace-loving policy. At the time of migration from Makkah, the idolaters were all set to wage war, but the

Prophet avoided this by quietly leaving his homeland for Madinah.

The mission of Islam is based on monotheism, its goal being to make people realize the existence of the one and only God and to strive to bring about a revolution in their hearts and minds in order that they may love God as is His due. And the greatest concern of man should be to fear and worship his Creator (2:165).

Peaceful circumstances produce a propitious environment for Islam, while violent circumstances result in antagonism towards it.

Such a *dawah* mission cannot afford wars and violent confrontations. When a state of war and violence prevails, the normal atmosphere is vitiated and such circumstances as would foster intellectual movements and spiritual reformation cannot be effectively created. It cannot be denied that peaceful circumstances produce a propitious environment for Islam, while violent circumstances inevitably result in antagonism towards Islam.

WAR: A STATE ACTION

In Islam, war is not the prerogative of the individual but of an established government. Only an established government can declare war. In other words, individuals can pray on their own, but they cannot wage wars of their own accord. Only when a war is declared by the ruling government, can the public join in and support it, and not before that. Islam does not sanction individual actions on this issue.

Quranic commands to do battle were always specific to particular sets of circumstances, and were not meant to be indiscriminately applied at the will of individuals.

As a general principle, the Quran tells us that, even where an external attack is feared, the common man should not act independently, but should take the matter to the ruler, then under his guidance take proper counter measures. (4:83).

The Hadith also states that 'the ruler is a shield, fighting is done under him, and security is attained through him.'

This clearly shows that the decision to do battle and its planning are the tasks of an established government. The common man can play his role as need be under government orders, and not independently.

This Islamic principle shows that there is no room for non-state warfare, which is what we generally call guerilla war. A guerilla war is fought by individual organizations, not by the State. As far as the state is concerned, if it wants to wage a defensive war against any country it has first—in obedience to the Quran—to issue a proper declaration. Only then can it wage a lawful war (8:58). In Islam, there is only 'declared' war. Therefore, in accordance with this principle, no proxy war in Islam can be lawful.

Targeting non-combatants even in defensive war is unlawful.

Most Islamic actions are governed by certain conditions. The waging of war is also thus subject to certain principles, one being that, even when a defensive war has been declared by the State, it will be aimed only at the combatants. Targeting non-combatants will be unlawful. The Quran enjoins us not to do battle with those who are not at war. Such people have to be dealt with kindly and equitably. But you are free to do battle with those who are fighting against you. (60:8-9)

According to Islam we can become martyrs, but we cannot court a martyr's death deliberately.

If, for instance, a Muslim state is at war with a particular nation, and this war is in conformance with Islamic principles, it should still not permit any destructive activities against non-combatants (civilians), as was done on September 11, 2001, in New York and Washington. Similarly in Islamic war, Muslims are not permitted to commit suicidal bombings in order to destroy the enemy. Strapping explosives on to oneself and hurling oneself upon the civilian settlements of even those with whom one is at war, for the purpose of destroying the enemy, and in the process killing oneself deliberately, is totally un-Islamic. This can in no way be termed *'shahadah'* (martyrdom). According to Islam we can become martyrs, but we cannot court a martyr's death deliberately.

The Difference Between the Enemy and the Aggressor

Under the scheme of the divine trial of human beings, man has been granted freedom by God. Due to this freedom, enmities may develop between people (20:123), which sometimes lead them to war. But Islam makes a clear difference between enmity and war.

Islam believes in turning one's enemy into a friend through peaceful means, instead of declaring him an enemy and then waging war against him.

Believers do not have the right to wage wars against their enemies. What the believers have to do as regards their enemies is far from waging war. Their duty is to peacefully convey to them the message of Islam. The Quran gives a clear injunction on this subject: "And good and evil deeds are not alike. Repel evil with good. And he who is your enemy will become your dearest friend." (41:33-34) That is to say, Islam believes in turning one's enemy into a friend through peaceful means, instead of declaring him an enemy and then waging war against him.

Islam does give permission to do battle. But such permission is given only in the case of an attack by opponents in spite of the policy of avoidance being followed by the Muslims, thus creating a situation where self-defence is required. The Quran has this to say: "Permission to take up arms is hereby given to those who are attacked because they have been wronged" (22:38). At another place the Quran gives a valid reason for fighting: "They were the first to attack you" (9:13).

This shows that according to the teachings of Islam, war is to be waged not against the enemy but against the aggressor. If Muslims hold someone to be their enemy, that does not give them the right to attack him. The one and only right given to them is to convey the peaceful message of Islam. Islam permits defensive fighting against violent aggression, but only when all efforts at avoidance and reconciliation have failed. The practical example of the Prophet Muhammad ﷺ provides an incontrovertible proof of the value of this policy.

The Power of Peace

According to a *hadith*, "God grants to gentleness what He does not grant to harshness." That is to say, peaceful activism is distinctly superior to violent activism. There is nothing mysterious about the point made in this *hadith*. It is a simple and a well-known fact of life that in a situation of war and violence, feelings of hatred and enmity flare up between the two sides and, in the process, the existing resources are destroyed. People from both sides get killed and the entire society turns into a jungle of negative feelings. It is quite obvious that in such an atmosphere no constructive and consolidated work can be done. There is nothing to be achieved in war and violence, save death and destruction.

"God grants to gentleness what he does not grant to harshness."

—The Prophet Muhammad

On the contrary, an atmosphere of peace enables

normal relations to be established between people. It makes it possible for feelings of love and friendship to prevail. In a favourable atmosphere constructive activities flourish and the existing resources can be used for development or other creative activities. A positive bent of mind will prevail which will help develop academic and intellectual advancement.

War brings nothing but death and destruction. Whereas peace fosters benign creativity.

The greatest ill-effect of war is that it limits human endeavour, whereas the greatest benefit of peace is that to the ultimate extent it opens up opportunities for improvement. War invariably results in further loss, while peace invariably results in further gain. That is why Islam teaches us to avoid war and confrontation at all costs and commands us to establish peace to the greatest possible degree.

Clarification of a Fallacy

There are certain verses in the Quran which convey injunctions similar to the following: 'Kill them wherever you find them.' (2:191)

Referring to such verses, there are some who attempt to give the impression that Islam is a religion of war and violence. This is totally untrue. Such verses relate in a restricted sense, to those who have unilaterally attacked the Muslims. The above verse does not convey the general command of Islam.

The truth of the matter is that the Quran was not revealed in the complete form in which it exists today. It was revealed from time to time, according to the circumstances, over a time span of 23 years. If this is divided into years of war and peace, the period of peace amounts to 20 years, while that of war amounts only to 3 years. The revelations during these 20 peaceful years were the peaceful teachings of Islam as are conveyed in the verses regarding the realization of God, worship, morality, justice, etc.

This division of commands into different categories is a natural one and is found in all religious books. For instance, the Gita, the holy book of the Hindus, pertains to wisdom and moral values. Yet along with this is the exhortation of Krishan to Arjun, encouraging him to fight. (3:30) This does not mean that believers in the Gita should wage wars all the time. Gandhiji, after all, derived his philosophy of non-violence from the same Gita. The exhortation to wage war in the Gita applies only to exceptional cases where circumstances leave no choice. But for general day-to-day existence it gives the same peaceful commands as derived from it by Mahatma Gandhi.

Similarly, Jesus Christ said: "Do not think that I came to bring peace on Earth. I did not come to bring peace, but a sword." (Matthew, Chapter 10)

It would not be right to conclude that the religion preached by Christ was one of war and violence, for such utterances relate purely to particular occasions. So far as general life is concerned, Christ taught peaceful values, such as the building up of a good character, loving each other, helping the poor and needy, etc.

The same is true of the Quran. When the Prophet of Islam emigrated from Makkah to Madinah, the idolatrous tribes were aggressive towards him. But the Prophet always averted their attacks by the exercise of patience and the strategy of avoidance.

However on certain occasions no other options existed, save that of retaliation. Therefore, he had do battle on certain occasions. It was these circumstances which occasioned those revelations relating to war. These commands, being specific to certain circumstances, had no general application. They were not meant to be valid for all time to come. That is why, the permanent status of the Prophet has been termed a 'mercy for all mankind.' (21:107)

The Qur'an states that the prophets were sent to the world as a mercy to the people (21:107).

Non-Violence and Islam

"We have sent you as a mercy for all the nations."
(The Quran, 21:107)

Non-violence should never be confused with inaction or passivity. Non-violence is action in the full sense of the word. Rather it is more forceful an action than that of violence. It is a fact that non-violent activism is more powerful and effective than violent activism. Non-violent activism is not limited in its sphere. It is a course of action which may be followed in all matters.

Whenever individuals, groups or communities are faced with a problem, one way to solve it is by resorting to violence. The better way is to attempt to solve the problem by peaceful means, avoiding violence and confrontation. Peaceful means may take various forms. In fact, it is the nature of the problem which will determine which of these peaceful methods is applicable to the given situation.

Islam is a religion which teaches non-violence. According to the Qur'an, God does not love *fasad*, violence. What is meant here by *fasad* is clearly expressed in verse 205 of the second chapter. Basically, *fasad* is that action which results in disruption of the social system, causing huge losses in terms of lives and property.

Those who seek to please God will be guided by Him to "the paths of peace". (16:5)

Conversely, we can say with certainty that God loves non-violence. He abhors violent activity in human society, as a result of which people have to pay the price with their possessions and even their lives. This is supported by other statements in the Qur'an. For instance, we are told in the Qur'an that Peace is one of God's names (59:23). Those who seek to please God are assured by verse 5 of the sixteenth *surah* that they will be guided by Him to "the paths of peace." Paradise, which is the final destination of the society of God's choice, is referred to in the Qur'an as "the home of peace" (89:30), etc.

The entire spirit of the Qur'an is in consonance with this concept. For instance, the Qur'an attaches great importance to patience. In fact, patience is set above all other Islamic virtues with the exceptional promise of reward beyond measure. (39:10)

Patience implies a peaceful response or reaction, whereas impatience implies a violent response. The word *sabr* exactly expresses the notion of non-violence as it is understood in modern times. That patient action is non-violent action has been clearly expressed in the Qur'an. According to one tradition, the Prophet Muhammad ﷺ observed: God grants to *rifq* (gentleness) what he does not grant to *unf* (violence). (Abu Dawud, *Sunan*, 4/255)

The Qur'an sets patience above all other Islamic virtues. Its reward is "beyond measure."

The word *rifq* has been used in this *hadith* as an antithesis to *unf*. These terms convey exactly what is meant by violence and non-violence in present times. This *hadith* clearly indicates the superiority of the non-violent method.

God's granting to non-violence what He does

not grant to violence is no simple matter. It has very wide and deep implications, embodying as it does an eternal law of nature. By this very law of nature, all bad things are associated with violence, while all good things are associated with non-violence.

Violent activities breed hatred in society, while non-violent activities elicit love. Violence is the way of destruction, while non-violence is the way of construction. In an atmosphere of violence, it is enmity which flourishes, while in an atmosphere of non-violence, it is friendship which flourishes. The method of violence gives way to negative values while the method of non-violence is marked by positive values. The method of violence embroils people in problems, while the method of non-violence leads people to the exploiting of opportunities. In short, violence is death, non-violence is life.

Violence is the way of destruction while non-violence is the way of construction.

Both the Qur'an and the Hadith have attached great importance to *jihad*. What is *jihad? Jihad* means struggle, to struggle one's utmost. It must be appreciated at the outset that this word is used for non-violent struggle as opposed to violent struggle. One clear proof of this is the verse of the Qur'an (25:52) which says: 'Perform *jihad* with this (i.e. the words of the Qur'an) most strenuously.'

Jihad with the Quran means an ideological struggle to conquer peoples' hearts and minds.

The Qur'an is a book of ideology. In such a case performing *jihad* with the Qur'an would mean an ideological struggle to conquer peoples' hearts and minds through Islam's superior philosophy.

In the light of this verse of the Qur'an, *jihad* in actual fact is another name for peaceful activism or non-violent activism. Where *qital* is violent activism, *jihad* is non-violent activism.

Peaceful Beginning

When the Qur'an began to be revealed, the first verse of the revelation conveyed the injunction: 'Read!' (*iqra*) (96:1). By perusing this verse we learn about the initiation of Islamic action. It begins from the point where there is hope of continuing the movement along peaceful lines, and not from that point where there are chances of its being marred by violence.

What are the advantages of non-violent activism over violent activism? They are briefly stated as under:

1. According to the Qur'an there are two faculties in every human being which are mutually antipathetic. One is the ego, and the other is the conscience, called respectively *nafs ammara* and *nafs lawwama* (The Qur'an, 12:53; 75:26). What the violent method invariably does is to awaken the ego, which necessarily results in a breakdown of social equilibrium. On the other hand, non-violent activism awakens the conscience. From this results an awakening in people of introspection and self-appraisal. And according to the Qur'an, the miraculous outcome of this is that "he who is your enemy will become your dearest friend." (41:34)

2. A great advantage of the non-violent method is that, by following it, no part of one's time is wasted. The opportunities available in any given situation may then be exploited to the fullest extent—

as happened after the no-war pact of Hudaybiyya. This peace treaty enabled the energies of the believers to be utilised in peaceful constructive activities instead of being dissipated in a futile armed encounter. One great harm done by violent activism is the breaking of social traditions in the launching of militant movements. Conversely, the great benefit that accrues from non-violent activism is that it can be initiated and prolonged with no damage to tradition.

The truly desirable revolution is that which permits gradual and beneficial changes. And this can be achieved only on the basis of non-violence.

Generally speaking, attempts to improve or replace existing systems by violent activism are counter-productive. One coup d'état is often the signal for a series of coups and counter-coups. The truly desirable revolution is that which permits gradual and beneficial changes. And this can be achieved only on the basis of non-violence.

Success Through the Non-Violent Method

All the great successes of the first phase of Islam as well as the succeeding periods were achieved by non-violent methods. Listed below are some examples of these successes.

1. Of the 23-year period of prophethood, the initial 13 years were spent by the Prophet in Makkah. The Prophet fully adopted the way of pacifism or non-violence during this time. There were many such issues in Makkah at that time which could have been the subject of clash and confrontation. But, sedulously avoiding all such issues, the Prophet Muhammad ﷺ strictly limited his sphere to peaceful propagation of the word of God. This resulted in *da'wah* work being performed in full force throughout this period. One of the great gains during these 13 years of *da'wah* work was the entry into the Islamic fold of men of the highest moral calibre, who were responsible for forming the history of Islam, for instance, Abu Bakr, Umar, Uthman and Ali, etc.

2. In Makkah when the Quraysh leaders were all set to wage war against the Prophet, even then, instead of opting for the way of reaction and

retaliation, what the Prophet did was to secretly migrate to Madinah.

Migration, by its very nature, was a clear example of non-violent activism. This peaceful strategy enabled the Prophet and his followers, about two hundred in number, to form a powerful centre of Islam in Madinah. Had they adopted the path of confrontation instead of peaceful migration, the history of Islam might have been buried right there in Makkah shortly after its inception.

Had the Prophet and his companions adopted the path of confrontation instead of peaceful migration, the history of Islam might have been buried shortly after its inception.

3. After the emigration, his antagonists took the unilateral decision to wage war against him. Consequently such bloody encounters as those of Badr and Uhud took place. Then the Prophet made a 10-year peace treaty known in history as Sulh al-Hudaybiyya, by accepting all the conditions of his opponents. This has been called a 'clear victory' in the Qur'an. It was this peace treaty,

paving the way for peaceful constructive activities which ultimately made possible the conquest of Makkah and the whole of Arabia.

4. At the end of the pious caliphate, a bloody encounter had taken place between the Banu Hashim and the Banu Umayyah. This stopped the advance of Islam for a period of ten years. What set this process in motion once again was the voluntary withdrawal of Hasan ibn Ali (d. 50 A.H.) from the battlefield. This was undeniably a practical form of non-violent activism. This peaceful move on the part of Hasan ibn Ali re-opened to Islam the locked doors of progress.

"The religion of Muslims has conquered where their arms had failed."

5. During the last days of the Abbasid caliphate Mongol tribes attacked the Muslim world and right from Samarkand to Aleppo destroyed the entire Muslim world. The history of Islam had apparently come to a standstill. At that moment the spirit of *da'wah* work was born within the Muslims. As a result, the majority of the Mongols converted to Islam. And that miracle took place which has been

described by an orientalist in these words: "The religion of Muslims has conquered where their arms had failed."

6. Islamic history took a crucial turn when, in the years succeeding the pious caliphate, rot had set in, in the system of the government, and the caliphate had turned into monarchy. At that juncture, many factors emerged which would have resulted in serious friction between the ruler and the ruled. But, following the guidance of the Prophet, the Muslims totally avoided political confrontation. This history, beginning with the Umayyad caliphate, continued for several centuries. This was possible because the *tabi'un* (companions of the Prophet's companions) and their succeeding generations, consisting of traditionists, jurists, *'ulama,* sufis and other great

All the precious books and the classical literature of Islam are a result of the peaceful activities during the time of the tabi'un and their succeeding generations.

religious scholars, all scrupulously avoided any clash or confrontation with the rulers.

It was during this period that, on the one hand, peaceful *da'wah* work was started in various countries, while on the other, the disciplines of Hadith, *fiqh* and other Islamic sciences came into existence on a large scale after a long period of great struggle. All the precious books which adorn our libraries, all the classical literature of Islam, are the result of these peaceful activities.

For instance, the Hadith as a source of *Shari'ah* is second only to the Qur'an in Islam. These traditions now exist in the form of printed books. These books are so precious that, without them, it would not have been possible to develop Islam into a complete system as it exists today. Under the rule of the Umayyads and Abbasids, when the political system had begun to deteriorate, where were these tens of thousands of traditions? All of them existed in the memory of the religious scholars, whose names are mentioned in the books as chains in the link of authorities who have handed this legacy down to us.

Had they adopted the principle of violent activism and clashed with the 'oppressive' rulers, they would all have been slaughtered by them and the entire legacy of traditions, instead of finding a place on the pages of books, would have been buried along with them in the graveyards. It is by the miracle of having adopted non-violence instead of violence that the precious sources of traditions have survived in book form and, till today, adorn our libraries.

Political Revolt Unlawful

Despite the blatant perversion in the Muslim rulers after the pious caliphate, the Muslim *ulama* did not lead an insurrection against these corrupt individuals. For about a period of one thousand years they remained detached in this matter and continued to engage all their efforts in non-political fields. This was not a matter of accident but in obedience to the express injunctions of the shariah.

As we know, in the books of Hadith detailed traditions have been set down in the chapters titled *Kitab al-Fitan*. The Prophet Muhammad ﷺ observed in plain words that in later times perversions would set in in the rulers, they would become tyrannical and unjust, but that Muslims should not wield their swords against them. They should rather move to the mountains with their goats and camels.

By 'goats and camels' are meant the opportunities in non-political fields which exist, even when the political institutions are corrupted. This injunction given by the Prophet meant that the Muslims should avail of such opportunities by avoiding clash and confrontation in the political field. In short, by ignoring the political problem, they should avail of the non-political opportunities.

These injunctions of the Prophet Muhammad ﷺ were so clear that the Muslim *ulama* of later times formed a consensus to make insurrection against the rulers unlawful.

Imam An-Nawawi, commenting upon some traditions as set forth by *Sahih Muslim* (*Kitab al-Imarah*) observes: "You should not come into conflict with the rulers in matters of their power. Even if you find them going against express Islamic injunctions, you should attempt to make the truth clear to them solely through words of wisdom and advice. So far as revolt and war against them in order to unseat them is concerned, that is totally unlawful according to the consensus of the *ulama*, even when the rulers are *zalim* and *fasiq* (tyrants and corrupt)." (*Sahih Muslim, bi sharh an-Nawawi*, 12/229)

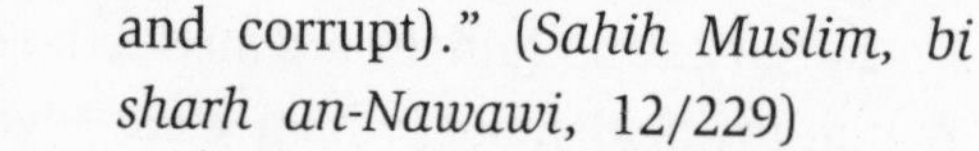

The Prophet forbade any uprising against political institutions. The resulting absence of strife permitted the uninterrupted propagation of Islam.

This command of the Prophet, as clearly expressed above, was based on extremely important considerations. In actual fact, in the early phase of Islam (as well as in the later phase) *da'wah* and reform works had to be performed, without which the history of Islam would not have been complete. If the *ulama* of the Muslim community had tried to pose a threat to the political institutions, certainly all this constructive work would have been left undone. That is why the Prophet Muhammad ﷺ expressly prohibited any clash with political institutions. This avoidance of strife guaranteed that non-political constructive work would continue to be performed without any break.

In every society there are always two systems side by side, one political and the other non-political. The latter is established through various non-political institutions. According to the scheme of Islam, non-political institutions established at the social level have always to remain stable. In this way there is a continuing endeavour—even when the political institutions have become corrupt, or keep changing—to keep Islam firmly established at the level of the non-political system.

There is no aggressive or offensive war in Islam. Islam allows only a defensive war and that, too, only when there is no other option.

The Command of War in Islam

It is a fact that certain verses in the Qur'an convey the command to do battle (*qital*) (22:39). What the special circumstances are which justify the issuance of and compliance with this command we learn from our study of the Qur'an.

1. The first point to be noted is that aggression or the launching of an offensive by the believers is

not totally forbidden. It is permissible, but with certain provisos. We are clearly commanded in the Qur'an: Fight for the sake of God those that fight against you, *but do not be aggressive.* (2:190)

2. Only defensive war is permitted in Islam. Such a war is one in which, as the Qur'an says: "They were the first to attack you." (9:13) i.e. aggression is committed by some other party so that the believers have to fight in self-defence. Initiating hostilities is not permitted for Muslims.

Furthermore, even in the case of the offensive being launched by an opposing group, the believers are not supposed to retaliate immediately. Rather in the beginning all efforts are to be made to avert war, and only when avoidance has become impossible, is battle to be resorted to in self-defence.

3. According to the Qur'an, there was one form of war which was time-bound strictly in relation to its purpose. This was to put an end to *fitna*. 'Fight against them until *fitna* is no more.' (2:193) In this verse *fitna* signifies that coercive system which had reached the extremes of religious persecution. In ancient times this coercive political system prevailed

all over the world. This absolutism had closed all the doors of progress, both spiritual and material. At that time God commanded the believers to break this coercive system in order to usher in freedom, so that all doors of spiritual and material progress might be opened to man.

According to the teachings of Islam, war is to be waged not against the enemy but against the aggressor.

Bringing monarchy to an end and establishing the caliphate in its place in the first phase of Islam was the beginning of this process. The system was first established in Arabia. At that time there were two major empires, the Byzantine and the Sassanid, to both of which the reform movement in Arabia posed a challenge. As a result, these empires wanted to crush it. The Prophet's companions therefore faced stiff resistance, but by God's succour they were successful in their mission and the coercive system, termed "absolute imperialism" by the French historian Henri Pirenne, was uprooted.

It took this revolutionary event to end a coercive system which had been established for centuries and replace it with a system based on freedom. This goal could not have been achieved in its first stage. But by divine succour Islam succeeded in breaking the historical continuity of this ancient coercive system in the 7th century. Subsequently, this change affected all of human history and as a continual process, ebbed and flowed until it reached its culmination in the 20th century. Then came the de-centralization which took place at the beginning of the 20th century, political power being limited solely to the administration. And the interference of political institutions became very limited. Social departments became generally independent of it.

This great change in the pattern of human life was exactly in accordance with Islam. It thus became possible for believers, whether they possessed political power or not to attain constructive goals without any hindrance. It was this system which effected the transition from the age of kingship to the age of institutions.

Thus it has become possible for the believers to set up various establishments of their own on a large scale, and indirectly bring political institutions under their influence. And in so doing, they can penetrate society, which was earlier possible only through political power: for instance, in training the new generation, creating an intellectual atmosphere by making available the print and electronic media, the propagation of ideas through books, continuing the process of *ijtihad* through research foundations, safeguarding religion by opening more mosques and schools, the acquisition of finance through industrial institutions, universal realization of one's objectives through the means of communication, realization of religious and cultural affairs through different channels, etc.

Jihad in actual fact is another name of peaceful activism or non-violent activism.

In modern time those nations who have understood this have achieved success even without having political power. Some have become established and excelled in the field of education, while others have set up empires in industry, communications or finance. The last in the list of these non-governmental empires is that of computers. This has given man the opportunity to keep his finger on the pulse of human activity not only at the national level, but also at the international level.

When the Quran says, "And religion is wholly for Allah" it portrays the most important aspect of the change of times. This change has reduced the status of political power to the point where it is no longer necessary for believers to wage a war for its acquisition, as it is no longer needed to secure the desired benefits. Non-political institutions serve this purpose equally well.

This mission was undertaken and brought to a successful conclusion at the internal level within Arabia during the life of the Prophet. Later, during the pious caliphate, the Sassanid and Byzantine empires were dismantled with special divine succour. Consequently, intellectual oppression at the international level was replaced by intellectual freedom.

In this connection those traditions are worth noting which are enshrined in *Sahih al-Bukhari*. When, after the fourth Caliph Ali ibn Abi Talib, political conflict ensued between Abdullah ibn Zubayr and the Umayyads, Abdullah ibn Umar, one of the seniormost companions of the Prophet, held himself aloof from the battle. People approached him and, quoting the verse of *qital-al-fitna*, asked him why he was not joining in the battle. Abdullah ibn Umar replied that *'fitna'* as mentioned in the Qur'an did not refer to political infighting, but rather to the religious coercive system, that had already been put an end to by them. (*Fathul Bari,* 8/60)

From this we learn that the war against *fitna* was a war of limited duration, temporary in nature, meant to be engaged in only until its specific purpose had been served.

Invoking the Qur'anic exhortation to do battle against *fitna* in order to validate acts of war which had quite other aims is highly improper. This verse could be cited only if the same state of affairs as existed at the time of its revelation, were to prevail once again.

The biographers of the Prophet Muhammad ﷺ have put the number of *ghazwah* (battle) at more than 80. This gives the impression that the Prophet Muhammad ﷺ in his 23-year prophetic career waged about four battles in a year. But this impression is entirely baseless. The truth is that the Prophet Muhammad ﷺ in his entire prophetic life, engaged in war only on three occasions. All the other incidents described as *ghazwat* were in actual fact examples of avoidance of war and not instances of involvement in battle.

For instance, in the books of *Seerah*, the incident of Al-Ahzab is called a *ghazwah* (battle), whereas the truth is that on this occasion the armed tribes of Arabia, twelve thousand in number, reached the borders of Madinah with all intentions of waging war, but the Prophet and his companions dug a deep trench between them, thus successfully preventing a battle from taking place. The same is the case with all the other incidents called *ghazwah*. The opponents of the Prophet repeatedly tried to embroil him in war, but on all such occasions, he managed to resort to some such strategy as averted the war, thus defusing the situation.

There were only three instances of Muslims really entering the field of battle—Badr, Uhud and Hunayn. But on all these occasions, war had become inevitable, so that the Prophet was compelled to encounter the aggressors in self-defence. Furthermore, these battles lasted only for half a day, each beginning at noon and ending with the setting of the sun. Thus it would be proper to say that the Prophet in his entire life span had actively engaged in war for a total of a day and a half. That is to say, the Prophet had observed the principle of non-violence throughout his 23-year prophetic career, except for one and a half days.

Believers do not have the right to wage wars against their enemies. Their duty is to peacefully convey to them the message of Islam.

The Islamic method, being based totally on the principle of non-violence, makes it unlawful for believers to initiate hostilities. Except in cases where self-defence has become inevitable, the Qur'an in no circumstance gives permission for violence.

The Modern Age and Non-Violence

The greatest problem facing Islam today is, as I see it, that Muslims have almost totally forgotten the *sunnah* (Prophet's way) of non-violence. In later times when the Ottoman and Mughal empires disintegrated and problems like that of Palestine have had to be confronted by the faithful, Muslims all over the world have fallen a prey to negative reaction on a colossal scale; they have failed to remember that the policy of Islam is not that of violence but of non-violence. It is the result of this deviation, that despite almost a 100 years of bloody wars, Muslims have achieved no positive gain. Rather whatever they already had has been lost by them.

According to Imam Malik, later generations of this *ummah* (Muslim community) will be able to settle matters at issue in the same way that earlier generations had done, i.e. by non-violent methods. Similarly, Muslims of modern times must likewise resort only to non-violent methods. Just as no gain could accrue from violent methods earlier, no gain can accrue from violent methods today.

The state of affairs of Muslims in modern times resembles that which prevailed at the time of Hudaybiyya. Today once again—only on a far larger scale—this *hamiyat al-jahiliya*, prejudices prevailing in pre-Islamic Arabia (48:28) is being displayed by the other party. In the first phase of Islam its solution lay in Muslims sedulously avoiding an equivalent display of prejudice, and in holding firmly to *kalima at-taqwa* (the word of piety) they became entitled to the succour of God and were granted a clear victory (48:26).

At the time of the Hudaybiyya peace treaty, the Quraysh, who had secured the leadership of Arabia, were bent on waging war. The Kabah was in their possession. They had expelled the Prophet and his companions from their home-town. They had taken possession of Muslims' homes and other properties, and spared no effort in disseminating negative propaganda against Islam.

Muslims can rewrite the history of Islam provided they make timely use of opportunities.

Given this state of affairs, there were only two options before the believers. One was to attempt to put an end to tyranny and launch an outright war on the other party in the name of securing their rights. The result of such a move would certainly have been further loss in terms of lives and property.

The second option was to remain patient in the face of immediate loss, be it political or material, and, in spite of the losses, avail of whatever opportunities were already available. The Prophet Muhammad ﷺ and his companions chose this second course. The result was that the entire history of Arabia was revolutionized in just a few years time.

The same state of affairs is widespread in modern times. Although today Muslims have suffered great losses, political and material, at the hands of other nations, there still exist a great number of opportunities on a far larger scale. If availed of wisely, we can rewrite the history of Islam in magnificent terms.

The Manifestation of Religion

The modern age is regarded by Muslims as being fraught with problems for Islam. But this is quite contrary to the actual situation. The modern age is in fact the age of Islam, just as the rainy season is the part of the year most benefical to farmers. But

Muslims, lacking in understanding and awareness, have failed to understand this; hence their failure to convert this potential into reality.

What is called *izhar ad-din* in the Qur'an does not refer to something which is temporary in nature. It, in fact, refers to an eternal ideological ascendancy of Islam. It means that in the world of ideology, such a revolution would be brought about as would establish the ideological supremacy of Islam forever. God has already brought it into existence potentially: believers have only to tap and convert this potential into reality.

Izhar ad-din signifies intellectual and ideological dominance, not political dominance.

The aim of the revolution brought about by the Prophet and his companions in the seventh century is stated to be *izhar ad-din* in the Qur'an:

> *They desire to extinguish the light of Allah with their mouths: but Allah seeks only to perfect His light, however much the disbelievers may abhor it (9:32-33).*

Izhar in Arabic means dominance/ascendancy/

supremacy. Here *izhar ad-din* signifies intellectual and ideological dominance, not political dominance. This means that in intellectual and ideological respects, God's religion assumes ascendancy over all other ideologies and religions for all time.

Granting ideological ascendancy to God's religion was no simple matter. It amounted to the writing of history afresh. For although God's religion had always been in a superior position ideologically, it had become obscured by false and misguided ideas, the reason being that in ancient times people were heavily under the influence of superstitious thinking. Their arts and learning in general had all become fettered by superstition and idolatry. This had led to a veil being thrown over true religion, which was the only vehicle for God's truth.

God desired that through the final Prophet an intellectual revolution be brought about which would alter this unfavourable and artificial state of affairs. Human sciences themselves have become supporters of the true religion so that, by academic standards themselves, the religion of monotheism may be made an established religion for the people.

Izhar ad-din in the above verse required this

same divine plan to be carried into effect through a revolution by the Prophet and his companions. This revolution set in motion a new process in human history. Its purpose was to unravel all the veils of superstition which clouded human judgement, and to lay bare the scientific proofs hidden in nature, so that the truth of monotheism could be brought to light for all humanity. In modern times this revolution has reached its culmination. There were two main aims of this *izhar ad-din*. One, that the system of religious persecution be put to an end, so that a propitious atmosphere could be created for the performance of *da'wah* of the true religion. In ancient times this task could be performed only in a very adverse atmosphere. The second purpose was to rally all arguments in support of God's true religion. Both these tasks have been performed on a large scale in present times. A brief mention of these is made here.

The latest scientific developments now uphold age-old religious truths.

In ancient times the monarchical system prevailed all over the world. An individualistic system like monarchy could be established by force alone. That is why a coercive system of governance was established by the monarchs. They inevitably crushed any sign of intellectual or religious freedom found among their subjects. This state of affairs posed a permanent obstacle to the general development of human thought or to the spreading of any religious mission. Ultimately this coercive political system was destroyed by the revolution brought about by the Prophet and his Companions.

The coercive and oppressive political system was destroyed by the revolution brought about by the Prophet and his companions which set in motion a process of intellectual liberalization.

This abolition of oppressive systems and the freeing of peoples' minds from superstition ushered in an era of freedom and democracy. The effect of this revolution in human history set in motion a process of intellectual liberalization. Later on western nations contributed greatly towards this revolution in human thought. Now this process has culminated in the unparalleled scientific achievements of the present day. In consequence, it has become possible for the task of *da'wah* of truth to be performed in an atmosphere of freedom, which was earlier seriously hampered by the oppressive atmosphere.

Idolatry is another name for a religion of superstitions. In ancient times this *shirk* (idolatry) dominated the minds of the people, having rendered the progress and development of science impossible. The Prophet and his Companions made great sacrifices to put an end to this superstitious system. In this way the age of science had its beginnings. The changes wrought by it influenced the course of history over the centuries.

The advent of the modern scientific age has made possible the global propagation of Islam for the first time in world history.

The scientific revolution, which was in actual fact a by-product of the Islamic revolution, gave us modern communications. The advent of this new age made it possible for the first time in human history for the propagation of Islam to be carried out on a universal scale. According to a *hadith* a time was to come when God's words would enter all the homes in the world. (*Musnad*, Ahmad) This was indirectly, a prediction of the modern age of communications.

One outcome of the modern scientific revolution is that we have at our disposal a number of new arguments in support of Islamic beliefs. Prior to this revolution the *da'is* of Islam could resort only to traditional arguments in support of the truth of Islam. But today it has become possible to measure up Islamic realities by the highest standards of human knowledge and to establish their authenticity by purely logical arguments.

According to a hadith, a time was to come when God's words would enter all the homes in the world (Musnad, Ahmad).

In ancient times religion could be studied only as something sacred and as a matter of dogma. That is why established and unestablished religions had not academically been distinguished from one another. In modern times, owing to the influence of the scientific revolution, the study of religions can be done as objectively and as critically as any other matter which comes under scientific scrutiny.

Such critical study has proved, purely academically, that by historical standards, there is only one reliable religion, and that is Islam. All other religions are lacking in this historical credibility. After this intellectual revolution it has become possible to establish the truth of Islam vis-à-vis other religions purely on the basis of human knowledge. That Islam is the only authentic version of divine religion may be fully supported by arguments.

Only under a normal relationship between the da'i and the mad'u, can the message of Islam be conveyed in a propitious atmosphere.

These modern developments in our times have taken Islam to the point of unopposed victory. Now the need of the hour is for Muslims to put an end unilaterally to all violent activities against *mad'u* nations, so that a normal relationship may be allowed to grow between *da'i* and *mad'u*: only then can the message of Islam be conveyed in a propitious atmosphere. Now, in the wake of the scientific revolution, it has become possible to begin a serious and beneficial dialogue between Islam and non-Islam, the result of which will necessarily be in favour of Islam.

Islam in the Present Age

Now the question arises as to whether an Islam which teaches non-violence can be of relevance in the present age, and assume a superior position once again in new situations.

The answer is entirely in the affirmative. The truth is that Islam's being a peaceful religion shows that it is an eternal religion. Had it been a religion of violence, it would not have been eternal. For, in modern times, the way of violence has been totally rejected by contemporary thinking. Now, only that system is worthy of consideration and acceptance the teachings of which are based on peace and non-violence.

Modern thinking, for example, has rejected communism. One of the major reasons was that communism had to be sustained by violence. And under no circumstances is violence acceptable to the modern mind. Nazism and Fascism too have been rejected on similar grounds. Modern man, therefore, disapproves of both religious and non-religious extremism, because they lead man ultimately to violence.

But Islam is a religion of nature. It has held violence as inadmissible from the outset. Islam has been an upholder of peace, not violence, from day one.

The time has come today for Islam to play a great constructive role, leading human history once again into a new age of progress.

In the past, Islam played a great role in the development of humanity, as a result of which human history entered a new age of progress and development. The time has come today for Islam to play a great constructive role, leading human history once again into a new age of progress.

What is called scientific or technical progress is the result of the discovery of some of the great secrets of nature. But if nature and its mysteries have always existed in our world, why has there been such a long delay in their discovery? Why could not the scientific advancement of the last few hundred years have been made thousands of years ago?

The reason was that in ancient times religion and science (divine knowledge and human knowledge) being so closely linked with one another, scientific enquiry was anathema to men of religion. Religious persecution had then become an insuperable obstacle to the progress of science.

Islam played a key role in disassociating religion from science. This paved the way for great progress to be made in the field of scientific investigation.

What Islam did was separate religion (which had become, in essence, a set of irrational beliefs) from scientific research and investigation. For instance, eclipses of the sun and moon had been linked with human destiny. The Prophet Muhammad ﷺ declared that eclipses had nothing to do with the lot of human beings. These were astronomical events, not events pertaining to the fate of mankind. (*Fathul Bari*, 2/611)

In this connection, an incident of the pollination

of dates is recorded in the books of Hadith how the Prophet of Islam observed that in worldly matters (such as the pollination of date palms) "you should act according to your experience, as you know these matters better." (*Sahih Muslim bi Sharh An-Nawawi*, 15/117)

This meant delinking religion and science from one another. In this way scientific research acquired an atmosphere of freedom for its functioning. For the first time in human history, science (human knowledge) could be developed freely without the intervention of religion. And advancing gradually, it culminated in the attainments of the modern age.

But today, man is again facing an even greater problem. That is, despite the extraordinary progress made in the field of science and technology, human beings are confronted with various kinds of problems, without there being any solution in sight. All these problems have resulted from not knowing the limit of freedom.

Modern man aspired to freedom as the highest good, but once having reached this goal, he was unable to set reasonable limits to freedom. In consequence, unrestrained freedom descended into anarchy and lawlessness. This is the actual cause of many of the problems which are emerging in modern times in western society. Now man requires an ideology which delimits his freedom, drawing the line between desirable and undesirable freedom. And it is only Islam which can provide him with such an ideology.

A dawah mission cannot afford wars and violent confrontations.

Now is the time for this ideology to be presented to man, who is ready and waiting to accept it. After the fall of communism (1991), the world is faced with an ideological vacuum. This vacuum can be filled by Islam alone. In the present world the developed countries have become economic or military superpowers, but the place is vacant for an ideological superpower, and that, potentially belongs to Islam.

There is only one obstacle in converting a great potential into a reality in favour of Islam. And that is the repeated recourse to violence by Muslim movements in modern times. Such action has presented Islam before the world in the guise of a violent religion. For this reason the man of today shies away from Islam. He fails to study Islam objectively. If this barrier could be removed and Islam once again brought before the world as a non-violent religion, or as a peaceful social system, then once again humanity would accept it, recognising it to be the voice of its own nature.

In the present world the developed countries have become economic or military superpowers, but the place is vacant for an ideological superpower, and that, potentially belongs to Islam.

Modern man is in need of a new religion or a new system, based on peace. It should be free from superstitious beliefs, and should provide the answers to deep psychological questions. Its principles should not clash with scientific realities.

Today no religion but Islam can lay such positive claims to acceptance, for it is Islam and Islam alone which fulfills all these conditions. Individually, there are many men and women today who, after having studied Islam, have acknowledged these unique qualities in Islam. Some have acknowledged them in theory while others have gone ahead and accepted Islam in practice.

THE TRUE JIHAD THROUGH *DA'WAH* ACTIVISM

Dawah proves Islam's ideological superiority. And without doubt nothing is greater than this. (10:32)

Islamic activism in respect of its method is based on non-violence and in respect of its target is based on *da'wah*. *Da'wah*, in fact, is another name for a peaceful struggle for the propagation of Islam. It would be true to say that Islamic activism in fact is *da'wah* activism.

The task of *da'wah* is no simple one. It enjoys the status of a key factor. If this task is fully performed, all other objectives will be automatically achieved. In support of this, here are certain quotations from the Qur'an:

1. Through *da'wah* the believers receive God's protection against the mischief of the opponents. (5:67)

2. Through *da'wah* even the direst enemy turns into one's dearest friend. (41:34)

3. *Da'wah* proves Islam's ideological superiority. And without doubt nothing is greater than this. (10:32)

4. Through *da'wah* a positive mentality is inculcated within the *ummah.* This is called 'honest counsel' in the Qur'an. (7:68)

5. The mission of *da'wah* is performed by human beings but the conditions conducive to its success are provided by God, just as the farming is to be done by the farmer while the rains come from God. In modern times favourable conditions have been fully provided to man. Now the believers' duty is to refrain from expending their energies in futile activities. They must exert their entire energy in *da'wah* work. All the best results will ensue from this act.

Peace and Justice

One great problem for Muslims is that peace does not necessarily guarantee them justice. This has caused Muslims to become violent and to neglect opportunities for *da'wah.* In modern times

Muslims want a peace which brings them justice. But according to the law of nature, this kind of peace can never be achieved, that is why Muslims the world over are in a state of physical and mental unrest. Distressed in their minds, they have become violent in their thinking and in their actions.

The truth is that peace does not automatically produce justice. Peace in actual fact simply opens up opportunities for the achievement of justice. At the time of Hudaybiyya the Prophet Muhammad ﷺ had not found justice. He had achieved peace but only by delinking it from justice. The Prophet had made this peace not to extract justice but to create opportunities for advancement. And, with the establishment of peace, great opportunities for *da'wah* action did open up which the Prophet exploited in full measure. Therefore, in just a few years' time the Prophet not only ensured justice, but set Islam upon a much more solid footing.

Peace in actual fact simply opens up opportunities for the achievement of justice.

The Muslims of the present day have to understand this secret of nature. Only then will it be possible for them first to find peace, then ultimately their desired goal of justice.

In October 1997, I met a 36-year old European, Leon Zippo Hayes, who was born in the city of Christchurch in New Zealand. After having studied Islam, he has changed his religion. His Islamic name is Khalilur Rahman. Passing through Muslim countries he is going to perform Hajj by land.

During the conversation he said that in modern times Muslims are engaged in bloody war at many places, at some places with others and at other places among themselves. This had led him (like many others) to conclude that perhaps Islam was a religion of violence. Later, he studied the Qur'an with the help of translations, and when he reached this verse in the Qur'an: 'Whoever killed a human being should be looked upon as though he had killed all mankind (5:32),' he said that he was so moved that he could not believe that it was there in the Qur'an.

This incident is broadly indicative of the thinking of non-Muslims on Islam. On seeing the actions of

Muslims, people today find it hard to believe that Islam may be a religion of peace. But if Muslims stop engaging in violent activities and give people the opportunity to appreciate Islam in its original form, then certainly a great number of people would realise, as they never had before, that Islam was a peaceful religion and they would rush to it, saying that it was exactly the religion which their souls had been seeking all along.

The Muslims have been unable to join the main-stream in modern times, it is because they are so easily provoked and so ready to resort to violence.

Muslims Displaced

It is an incontrovertible fact that Muslims have not been able to join the mainstream in modern times. At all places and in every department they are leading their lives as if driven into a corner. This is undoubtedly an extremely critical problem, for it has relegated Muslims to second class positions all over the world.

To me, the greatest reason for this is the violent attitude of the Muslims. Today's Muslims are easily provoked and become violent at anything which is against their way of thinking. Not all Muslims become involved in acts of violence. Yet all might be held culpable. This is because that section of Muslims—in fact, the majority—who are not personally involved, neither disown those members of their community who are engaged in violence, nor even condemn them. In such a case, according to the Islamic *Shariah* itself, if the involved Muslims are directly responsible, the uninvolved Muslims are also indirectly responsible.

If you behave properly with those holding divergent views from you, then you deserve to be credited with having an excellent character.

It is Muslims' religious and secular leaders who are actually responsible for this violent approach on the part of Muslims today. In modern times when Muslims have had to undergo the experience of defeat, almost all the religious and secular scholars as well as intellectuals followed one single line, that of awakening the spirit of *jihad* (in the sense of *qital*) among Muslims. The entire Muslim world reverberated with such slogans as '*jihad* is our way' and '*Jihad* is the only solution to our problems!'

The entire world has witnessed a great number of large and small movements in violent response to the problems faced by Muslims. If you go to Palestine, you will hear young people singing a song, no doubt taught to them by their elders:

> Let's make war, let's make war,
> For war is the way to success.

In modern times, the violent approach of our intellectuals and leaders of movements, is the sole reason for the present violent mentality among Muslims all over the world. It is as a result of this mentality that, if anyone writes a book against Islam, Muslims are prepared to kill him. If any procession raises anti-Muslim slogans, Muslims start stoning the procession instead of killing the evil by observing silence, which, as Umar Faruq advocated, would be the best strategy in such a case. If there is any monetary or territorial controversy with any nation, they immediately take up arms against it, rather than adopt a peaceful strategy to solve the problem.

This violent mentality of Muslims is responsible for having alienated them from their neighbours everywhere. Their conduct clearly shows that they no longer cherish the ideal of universal brotherhood. Everywhere they are looked upon with aversion and dread. The resulting dissociation has left Muslims a backward group in modern times. Even in advanced countries like America they remain backward as a community in comparison with other immigrant groups.

Let Muslims once renounce violence and they will be welcomed, as brothers, into the main-stream. In all institutions ranging from the social to the edu-cational, the equality of their partnership will be assured.

The only way to alleviate the tragic plight of Muslims is to bring them back to non-violent Islam, by helping them to understand that their violent version of Islam is not the true one.

As soon as Muslims take to the path of non-violent Islam, they will be able to become equal partners with other communities. They will have joined the universal mainstream, and will consequently be able to participate in all activities, in all institutions. People, instead of dreading them, will welcome them in every field. They will become a part of the universal brotherhood. Their issues will be looked upon with justice. Their equal partnership will be assured in all institutions ranging from the social to the educational.

Violent activities breed hatred in society, while non-violent activities foster love.

Peaceful interaction will give Muslims the kind of intellectual stimulation and variety of experience which they must have if they are to tread the path of progress. Interaction will also facilitate the task of *da'wah* on a large scale. The natural result of this vast interaction of Muslims and non-Muslims will be that everywhere dialogue on Islam will be started, formally as well as informally. In modern times, because of the extremist and violent attitude of Muslims, serious dialogue between Islam and non-Islam has almost come to an end. Now when peaceful interaction between Muslims and non-Muslims takes place in a normal atmosphere, serious dialogue will ensue on its own. The beginning of serious dialogue between Islam and non-Islam is, without doubt, a very great success from the point of view of *da'wah.*

The Qur'an describes *Sulh al-Hudaybiyya*, in the early period of Islam as a 'clear victory'. It was a 'clear victory' in the sense that it established peace between the believers in monotheism *(tawhid)* and believers in polytheism *(shirk)*, thus making it possible for a serious dialogue to be held between the two on religious matters.

Muslims themselves must show the rest of the world that Islam is a religion of peace.

In modern times if Muslims abandon the path of violence and fully adopt the path of non-violence, this will be for Muslims like reviving the *sunnah* of Hudaybiyya. And they will start receiving great benefits, similar to those which Islam and Muslims had gained after the event of Hudaybiyya in the first phase.

Tolerance!! Its Significance Today

"Requite evil with good..."
(Qur'an, 23:96)

On January 1st, 1995, newspapers flashed the news that "the United Nations has proclaimed 1995 as the 'Year of Tolerance,'" saying that the ability to be tolerant of the actions, beliefs and opinions of others is a major factor in promoting world peace. Amidst the resurgence of ethnic conflicts, discrimination against minorities and xenophobia directed against refugees and asylum-seekers, tolerance is the only way forward, said the statement of the United Nations Educational, Scientific and Cultural Organisation, (UNESCO). It is said, racism and religious fanaticism in many countries had led to many forms of discrimination and the intimidation of those who held contrary views. Violence against and intimidation of authors, journalists and others who exercise their freedom of expression, were also on the increase along with political movements which seek to make particular groups responsible for social ills such as crime and unemployment. Intolerance is one of the greatest challenges we face on the threshold to the 21st century said the UNESCO Statement. Intolerance is both an ethnic and political problem. It is a rejection of the differences between individuals and between cultures. When intolerance becomes organised or institutionalised, it destroys democratic principles and poses a threat to world peace.

The ability to be tolerant of the actions, beliefs and opinions of others is a major factor in promoting world peace.

—The United Nations

This proclamation of the U.N. is most apt and timely. The prime need of the world today is indeed tolerance.

One of the stark realities of life is that divergence of views does exist between man and man, and that it impinges at all levels. Be it at the level of a family or a society, a community or a country, differences are bound to exist everywhere. Now the question is how best unity can be forged or harmony brought about in the face of the human tendency to differ.

In this world, unity is achievable only by learning to unite inspite of differences, rather than insisting on unity without differences.

Some people hold that the removal of all differences is the sine qua non for bringing about unity. But, this view is untenable, as it is not practicable. You may not like the thorns which essentially accompany roses, but it is not possible for you to pluck out all the thorns and destroy them completely. For, if you pluck out one, another will grow in its place. Even if you run a bull-dozer over all rosebushes, new plants will grow in their place which will bear roses ineluctably accompanied by thorns. In the present scheme of things, roses can be had only by tolerating the existence of thorns. Similarly, a peaceful society can be created only by creating and fostering the spirit of tolerance towards diversities. In this world, unity is achievable only by learning to unite in spite of differences, rather than insisting on unity without differences. For their total eradication is an impossibility. The secret of attaining peace in life is tolerance of disturbance of the peace.

There is nothing wrong in diversity of opinions. In fact, this is a positive quality which has many advantages. The beauty of the garden of life is enhanced if the flower of unity is accompanied by the thorn of diversity.

An advantage flowing from this attitude is that it builds character. If you are well-mannered towards those whose views are similar to yours, you may be said to exhibit a fairly good character. But, if you behave properly with those holding divergent views from you or who criticise you, then you deserve to be credited with having an excellent character.

In the same way, a society whose members hold identical views and never have any controversial discussions, will soon find itself in the doldrums. The intellectual development of the members of this society will be frozen, because personal evolution takes place only where there is interaction of divergent thinking. So where there is no such interaction, how can there be intellectual development?

The adoption of a policy of tolerance in the face of controversy and opposition is not a negative step. It is undoubtedly a positive course of action.

Divergence of views plays an important role in the development of the human psyche. It is only after running the intellectual gauntlet that a developed personality emerges. If in a human society, this process ceases to operate, the development of character will come to a standstill.

Nobody in this world is perfect. If a man is endowed with some good qualities, he may be lacking in others. This is one of the reasons why differences crop up among people. But, for life as a whole, these differences are actually a great blessing: the good points of one man may compensate for the shortcomings of another, just as one set of talents in one man may complement a different set in another. If people could only learn to tolerate others' differences, their very forbearance would become a great enabling factor in collective human development.

The habit of tolerance prevents a man from wasting his time and talent on unnecessary friction. When negatively affected by another's unpalatable behaviour, your mental equilibrium is upset. But if you remain emotionally untouched by such behaviour, your mind will fully retain its equilibrium and, without wasting a single moment, you will continue to perform your work in the normal way. The policy of tolerance or forbearance enhances your efficacy, while intolerant behaviour reduces it.

Forbearance is a great enabling factor in collective human development.

Tolerance is not an act of compulsion. It is a positive principle of life, expressing the noble side of a man's character. The existence of tolerant human beings in a society is just like the blooming of flowers in a garden.

Tolerance: The Price of Peace

We cannot have anything in this world without paying for it. Everything has its price and this is particularly true of peace. If we want peace, we should be ready to pay for it or stand deprived of it. What is the price of peace? It is simply tolerance. We live in a world of differences, and these differences cannot be eliminated. Therefore, we have only two options before us: adopting the policy of either tolerance or intolerance. While the latter leads to violence, the former ensures peace. Where there is tolerance there is peace, and where there is intolerance, there is war and violence. There is only one universal formula of tolerance for peace, and this same formula may be successfully applied to one's family life and to social life, as well as at the international level.

The root cause of most of our problems is traceable to our deviation from the peaceful model of nature.

Peace requires us to foster a culture of tolerance, for intolerance can lead only to war.

In the present world the root cause of most of our problems is traceable to our deviation from the peaceful model of nature—the best model for us to follow. All the dilemmas we are facing today arise because we have not followed nature's lead.

Human beings should follow the example of the stars and planets which remain in continual motion in their orbits, without ever colliding with one another.

The stars and planets are in continual motion in their orbits, but they never collide with one another. This serves to show man how to proceed to his destination in life without coming into conflict with others. The sun too is an excellent model. It shows us how we should give life to others in a totally undiscriminating way. The tree is also a shining example to man, in supplying healthy and beneficial oxygen in exchange for harmful gas, that is, carbon dioxide. And just look at how the flowers spread fragrance all around, regardless of whether they are appreciated for it or not. A flowing stream is likewise a model when it irrigates the fields without expecting anything in return. Without the inculcation of these altruistic values among human beings, no meaningful life on earth is possible.

Peace is essential for a better way of living—peace of mind, peace in the family and peace in nature.

In short, positivity prevails throughout Nature. Negativity just does not exist in the natural world. This teaches us the lesson that we should give a positive response at all times, even in negative situations.

Christ has exhorted us to follow Nature's example in these divine words: 'Our Father in Heaven! Hallowed be Your name, Your Kingdom come, Your Will be done, on earth as it is in Heaven.' (Matthew, 6:10)

Conclusion

Peace is the only religion for both man and the universe. In a peaceful environment all good things are possible, whereas in the absence of peace, we cannot achieve anything of a positive nature, either as individuals, or as a community. The same holds true at national and international levels.

Scholars have rightly defined peace as "the absence of war" However, there are some who hold that peace should necessarily be accompanied by justice. But setting such a condition for the attainment of peace is impractical. For the role of peace is purely to set the stage for us to strive for justice and to work towards other constructive ends.

The Prophet Muhammad ﷺ provides a very clear example in his method of negotiating the Hudaybiyya peace treaty. By unilaterally accepting the conditions of his opponents, he concluded a historic 10-year no-war pact, without apparently receiving justice or his rights. But by means of this peace treaty the Prophet and his companions were enabled to consolidate themselves so thoroughly that they had no need to wage war to attain justice.

Japan abandoned violence and adopted a peaceful course which helped it become a great economic super power.

Japan's industrial cities, Hiroshima and Nagasaki, were destroyed by atom bombs in 1945. After the holocaust, Japan abandoned violence and adopted a peaceful course that it termed a "reverse course" for its national development. Consequently, within forty years, without any return to militarism, Japan became a great economic superpower.

Violence and peace both have wide connotations. Violence is a concomitant factor in everything from personal hatred to all-out war, whereas peace is marked by every positive virtue from tolerance to love. Peace is synonymous with normalcy, and normalcy provides all such opportunities as favour the growth of a healthy environment. All kinds of achievements are possible in an ambience of peace. While peace is a boon for human society, violence is a curse. Peace and love go hand in hand while hatred breeds violence. Peace brings people closer, while violence tears them asunder. Peace fosters a high level of human outlook, whereas violence breeds a jungle outlook. Peace promotes life, while violence is the harbinger of death and destruction. Peace brings the good elements of a society into prominence, while violence does quite the reverse.

Christ once said, "Love your enemy." This means to be on peaceful terms with one's enemy, i.e. winning over your enemy by using the power of peace. This is the divine formula to attain peace.

The religious viewpoint on this subject is very aptly conveyed in the Qur'an: "God calls to the Home of Peace."(10:25) This means that according to the creation plan, peace and harmony should prevail in human society. God Himself is Peace (Peace being an attribute of God). He intended this world to be peaceful, and only a peaceful world will be able to receive His blessings.

A peaceful world is like a paradise on earth. It is only in such a world that we can meet and establish contact with God, the Creator of Man and the Universe.

A peaceful world is like a paradise on earth. It is only in such a world that we can meet and establish contact with God, the Creator of Man and the Universe.

No excuse, therefore, justifies the use of violence, in individual or national life. We must maintain peace unilaterally, for nothing that we desire can be achieved without it.

Although at opposite poles, peace and violence result from human thinking. And if one were to think of the end result, one would never indulge in violence. One should bear in mind that peace is in consonance with humanity, whereas violence means a descent to the animal level. Peaceful minds make for a peaceful world. Man was born in peace. Man must die in peace.

A Guide for
THE YOUNG
MUSLIM

A Guide for
THE YOUNG
MUSLIM

A Guide for
THE YOUNG
MUSLIM

THE ARABIC
ALPHABET
THE BEAUTIFUL NAMES OF ALLAH

Bouquet
of the Noble
Hadith

Forty
Hadith

SERMONS
MUHAMMAD

A HISTORY OF
ARABIC
LITERATURE

ISLAMIC ART
ARCHITECTURE

After Death,
Life!

Introducing
Islam
A Simple Introduction to Islam

INDIAN
MUSLIMS
The Need For A
Positive Outlook

PRINCIPLES OF
Islam

Vision

Tabligh
Movement

WORDS
PROPHET
MUHAMMAD
SELECTIONS FROM
THE HADITH

HANDBOOK
MUSLIM
BELIEF

Islamic
Thought
and its Place
in History

THE MIRACLE
IN THE ANT

THE MIRACLE OF
CREATION IN PLANTS

THE MIRACLE
IN THE SPIDER

Death
Resurrection
Hell
HARUN YAHYA

ALLAH IS
KNOWN
THROUGH
REASON

TIMELESSNESS AND
THE REALITY OF
FATE

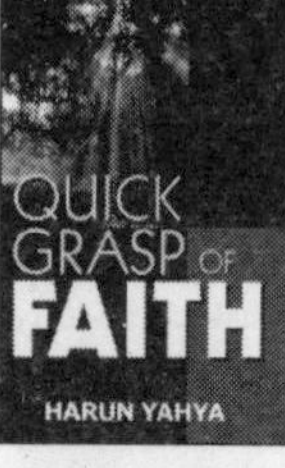
QUICK
GRASP OF
FAITH
HARUN YAHYA

THE MIRACLE
OF THE
IMMUNE SYSTEM

CRUDE
UNDERSTANDING
DISBELIEF
HARUN YAHYA

HARUN YAHYA
EVER
THOUGHT
TRUTH?

THE
MORAL
VALUES
QURAN
HARUN YAHYA

ETERNITY HAS
ALREADY
BEGUN

The
Basic
Concepts
in the
Quran
HARUN YAHYA

MUSLIM
PRAYER

The Blessings of
RAMADAN
Javed Ali

Tell Me About
MUHAMMAD

Tell Me About
MUSA

Tell Me About
CREATION

THE STORY OF THE PROPHET YUSUF

THE MOST BEAUTIFUL NAMES OF
ALLAH
SAMIRA FAYYAD KHAWALDEH

Ibn Battuta
H.A.R. GIBB

Humayun Nama
Gul-Badan Begam

THE STORY OF
ISLAMIC SPAIN
SYED AZIZUR RAHMAN

ISLAM
AT THE
CROSSROADS
MUHAMMAD ASAD

DECISIVE MOMENTS
IN THE
HISTORY
OF
ISLAM
MUHAMMAD ABDULLAH ENAN

Islamic
Medicine
EDWARD G. BROWNE

Spanish Islam
A History of the Muslims in Spain
REINHART DOZY

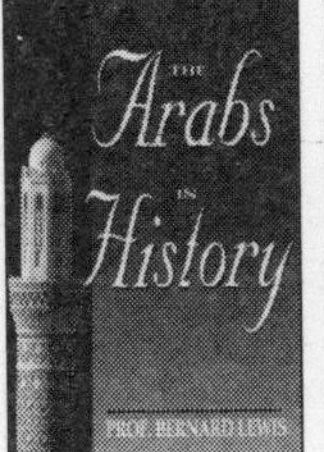
THE
Arabs
IN
History
PROF. BERNARD LEWIS

ARABIC ENGLISH DICTIONARY
J.G. HAVA

How Greek Science Passed to the Arabs
De Lacy O'Leary

THE HOLY
QUR'AN

The Pilgrimage to
MAKKAH

One
RELIGION

ISLAMIC
THOUGHT
S. WAQAR AHMAD HUSAINI

A Dictionary of
Muslim
Names

The Travels of
Ibn Battúta
H.A.R. GIBB

ISLAM
REDISCOVERED

THE
SPREAD
OF
ISLAM
IN THE WORLD
A History of Peaceful Preaching
Prof. Thomas Arnold

The Travels of
Ibn Jubayr
Roland Broadhurst

The
Story of the
Prophet Nuh
Quran Stories for Tiny Tots

A HISTORY OF
ARABIAN MUSIC
HENRY GEORGE FARMER

Quran
Astronomy
Earth Exploration from Space
S. Waqar Ahmed Husaini

Children's Stories from the Quran
The Ark of Nuh
and the Great Flood
Sticker Book

GCSE
ISLAM
The Do-It-Yourself Guide
Ruqaiyyah Waris Maqsood

GOD
ARISES
MAULANA WAHIDUDDIN KHAN

THE MORISCOS OF
SPAIN
HENRY CHARLES LEA